PPS
PRODUCTIVE
PROBLEM
SOLVING

Robert R. Carkhuff, Ph.D.
CARKHUFF INSTITUTE OF HUMAN TECHNOLOGY

Copyright © 1973, 1985 by
Human Resource Development Press, Inc.

22 Amherst Rd.
Amherst, Masasachusetts 01002 (413) 253-3488
1-800-822-2801

Bernice R. Carkhuff, Publisher
Elizabeth Grose, Editor

Library of Congress Cataloging in Publication Data
International Standard Book Number 0-87425-019-6

Cover Design by Dorothy Fall
Word processing by Susan Kotzin
Composition by Magazine Group
Printing and Binding by Bookcrafters

ABOUT THE AUTHOR

Dr. Robert R. Carkhuff is the most-referenced counseling psychologist according to Division 17, American Psychological Association. He is Chairman, Carkhuff Institute of Human Technology, a non-profit institute dedicated to the development and implementation of human resource development, training and performance programs in home, school, work and community settings.

The American Institute for Scientific Information ranks Dr. Carkhuff as the second youngest of the 100 most-cited social scientists, including such historical figures as Dewey, Freud and Marx. He is also author of three of the 100 most-referenced texts, including his two-volume classic, *Helping and Human Relations*.

Dr. Carkhuff is known as the originator of helping models and human resource development skills programs. He is also parent of the Human Technology™ movement which emphasizes models, systems and technologies for individual performance and organizational productivity. His most recent books on the topics of human resource development and productivity are *Sources of Human Productivity* and *The Exemplar; the Exemplary Performer in the Age of Productivity*.

PREFACE

Problem-solving is one of the skills essential to effective human functioning. The ability to resolve problems ensures our survival, and increases our chances for growth.

But productive problem-solving requires determination and a sense of responsibility in our lives. Solving problems efficiently and effectively can be a challenge, although it is a rewarding process.

Productive Problem-Solving presents a model that addresses that challenge; it is based upon *The Art of Problem Solving,* first published more than a decade ago, and used by tens of thousands of readers. This model has relevance for individuals as well as groups and institutions, for if we can solve problems as individuals, then we can conquer group problem-solving.

Productive Problem-Solving has special significance for parents, teachers, counselors and administrators— for all of us who recognize the importance of problem-solving to productivity and growth.

With productive problem-solving skills, we can encourage the conditions which nurture human and community development, while living our individual lives more fully.

Washington, D.C.   R.R.C.
May, 1985

PPS
PRODUCTIVE PROBLEM SOLVING

Table of Contents

APPENDIX

A Father's Problem Solving

John had a problem. He was a deeply religious person who had to make a critical career decision in the twilight of his priesthood years. A scholar of some note, he had to choose between several careers in teaching. Somehow, none seemed to satisfy his overriding spiritual value: he wanted to know whether what he was doing was consistent with the will of God. He believed this value to be beyond operational definition in the world of humans. He entered the problem-solving process. When he explored his experience, he came to understand the significance of the time dimension for him. Further analysis led him to focus upon communicating with God. He expanded his career alternatives to include personal counseling as well as teaching. He defined his values in terms of being able to pray for five minutes each hour. He evaluated the career courses in terms of their impact upon this value and chose his preferred career course— counseling. Counseling provided the "fifty-minute hour" which allowed for his prayer and meditation. He further improved this course by including spiritual as well as personal counseling. That way, he could work to help others define their spiritual relationship with God. John considered his solution to be ideal. It promised to bring him in closer communion with God.

This simple story illustrates the principles of productive problem-solving: exploring and understanding the problem; analyzing the critical dimensions of the problem; expanding alternative courses of action; defining values operationally; evaluating the courses of action in terms of their impact upon the values; choosing and improving the preferred courses of action. The problem-solving process recycles human experience in a never-ending attempt to improve the quality of human life—and in John's case, spiritual life.

Perhaps the larger issue revolves around John's experience. His spiritual values, he initially felt, defied operational definition. Yet in their definitions and implementation in problem-solving, he was freed to pursue still higher levels of spirituality. If we can define the problem-solving process in complex spiritual matters, how much can we do with problems in everyday living, learning and working? With free people, there are no problems beyond resolution, provided the people have skills in problem-solving.

1
INTRODUCTION

Problems are universal. Everyone has problems every-day. We have small problems and big problems. Small problems may include balancing checkbooks, fixing cars, visiting teachers. Big problems may include selecting or leaving spouses, schools and careers. At the time any problem may appear to be a big problem. This is especially true when we reach the point of frustration with new problems heaped upon old problems.

Problems are Universal

Productive Problem-Solving

Problems involve taking on responsibilities. It seems that the older we get, the more problems we have. The more responsibilities we have, the more problems we must resolve. Indeed, it would appear that the more problems we solve, the more problems we accept responsibility for. For young people, life seems to be a process of being rewarded for doing something good. Mature people recognize that life is a process of receiving more responsibilities for those responsibilities discharged.

Problems Involve Taking Responsibilities

Problems are cumulative. Those problems which we do not resolve accumulate in larger and larger problems. They have a "snowballing" effect. Sooner or later, they become overwhelming. In order to prevent the accumulation of problems, we must learn to intervene to resolve the problems. By intervening effectively and efficiently, we reduce the potency of the problems.

Problems are Cumulative

Problems have implications. How we intervene determines our results. Problem-solving may be for better or worse. If we learn to resolve problems productively, we can actually transform our deficits into assets. Seen in this light, problems become opportunities to improve ourselves. If we do not learn to resolve problems productively, our deficits may become increasingly handicapping and destructive.

Problems Have Implications

The secret to living productively is to learn productive problem-solving. Productive problem-solving involves finding the solution that does two things: maximizes the human benefits; minimizes the resource investments. Productive problem-solving is itself both effective and efficient. It is a process that emphasizes finding the most economical way to produce the most beneficial solution.

Productive Problem-Solving

PPS Skills

The productive problem-solving (PPS) process involves several sets of skills. First, we must understand the problem by processing information about it. Second, we must analyze the problem by breaking it down into its component dimensions. Third, we must develop alternative courses of action in order to solve the problem. Fourth, we must define our values in order to study the impact of the alternative courses. Fifth, we must choose the preferred course of action based upon the most positive impact upon our values. Sixth, we must attempt to improve the preferred alternative.

Understanding the problem emphasizes processing information about it. This means, first, preparing for problem-solving by attending to sources of information about the problem. Secondly, it means exploring the parameters of the information. Third, it means understanding the implications of the problem for the person. Thus, at the highest levels of understanding, the problem-solver personalizes the problem for himself or herself. In doing so, the problem-solver assumes responsibility for his or her role in the problem. Moreover, the problem-solver assumes responsibility for doing something about the problem. (Understanding the problem is the topic of Chapter 2.)

"I feel disappointed in myself because I cannot manage my situation, and I'm really eager to be able to manage it."

Understanding the Problem

Analyzing the problem emphasizes breaking it down into its component parts. The parts of the problem include the components, themselves, i.e., *who* and *what* is involved. The parts also include the functions which we are trying to accomplish, i.e., *what* we are trying to do. The parts of the problem also include the processes by which we attempt to accomplish the functions, i.e., *why* and *how* we are trying to do it. Also included are the conditions of the problem, i.e., *where* and *when* we are trying to do the things. Finally, the parts of the problem emphasize the standards of performance, i.e., *how well* we are expected to do. Problems are made up of deficits in one or more of these component parts. Goals are a synthesis of these very same dimensions.

"The way I see it, I just haven't been able to live up to the standards of performance expected of me."

Analyzing the Problem

Developing the alternative courses of action emphasizes the different ways available to us to resolve the problem. First, there are the "Go/No Go" solutions that most people use. Either we do it or we don't! Usually, these apparent solutions compound the original problem by generating other larger problems. In between these extreme solutions are a seemingly infinite number of alternative courses of action. Usually these potential solutions involve one or more of the following ingredients: people solutions, program solutions, organizational solutions.

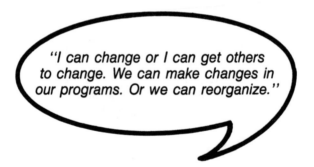

"I can change or I can get others to change. We can make changes in our programs. Or we can reorganize."

Developing Alternative Courses

Defining our values is the most important **PPS** skill. Values are the meanings we attach to people, data or things. Defining our values enables us to ask and answer the basic question in problem-solving: what do we want to get out of this situation and what are we willing to do to get those benefits? Usually, values are conceived of in terms of the benefits we are hoping to achieve. However, values must also be conceived of in terms of the resources we are willing to invest. Generally, we are trying to maximize our benefits while we minimize our costs.

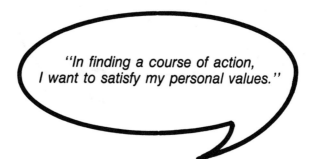

"In finding a course of action, I want to satisfy my personal values."

Defining Values

Choosing a preferred course of action emphasizes finding that course which best satisfies our values. Usually, the preferred course of action is the same as the most productive course of action. The most productive course of action is that course of action which maximizes our benefits and minimizes our costs.

"My best course is my most productive course!"

Choosing Preferred Courses

Improving courses of action emphasizes upgrading the benefits and downgrading the resource investments. In other words, improving courses of action involves modifying the courses so they become increasingly productive. We improve courses of action by comparing them with the benefits of potentially ideal solutions. Then we reconfigure the courses in order to incorporate the best attributes which are not mutually exclusive.

"My best course can always be improved!"

Improving Courses

Productive problem-solving is a life-long process. Given the constantly changing environment of the Information Age, we continuously find ourselves in new situations. As a consequence, we are always processing new information in order to understand the problem. We are constantly analyzing and reanalyzing problems in terms of their component parts. We are developing new and exciting courses of action. We are defining and redefining our values. We are constantly choosing and improving preferred and productive courses of action. In an age of constant change, we are continuously changing. In an age of mushrooming problems, we are becoming more productive in both resolving the problems and benefiting from the resolution of the problems.

Productive Problem-Solving

2
UNDERSTANDING
THE PROBLEM

Ann had a problem; in fact, she had many problems. Ann was a mother of four and a serious homemaker. She was a teacher, a graduate student, and many other things. Ann functioned in many roles, and she took them all very seriously. Indeed, at this moment in time, she felt overwhelmed. Ann could be heard saying with growing frequency: "I'm tired—there simply aren't enough hours in the day for me to do what I have to do." Increasingly, she was afraid of losing control of her situation. To resolve her problem, Ann needed to address its sources, explore her experience, and understand her goals.

UNDERSTAND GOALS

EXPLORE EXPERIENCE

ATTEND TO SOURCES

Understanding

At first, Ann asked many people for help. She asked relatives and friends. She asked colleagues and associates. She asked neighbors. She even asked strangers she met on the bus. Somehow, she felt there was something missing in all of their suggestions or prescriptions. There was something of herself missing. None of them really understood her. Finally, in desperation, she sought professional help. But even this experience was disappointing.

Ann began to feel panicked. She felt her energy draining from her. She knew that she must do something now or soon it might be too late. Her problems were moving incessantly from crisis to catastrophe. She feared a tragedy was inevitable.

"What should I do?"

Problems Lead to Desperation

Everyone seemed to offer a different solution. It all became so very confusing. Just when it seemed like one suggestion made sense, someone would make another, and some of them were very good suggestions. For example, for a while Ann seriously considered getting child care for two of her children who were of pre-school age. Several persons suggested this course and it seemed like a good idea while she was talking with them. But something seemed to prevent her from taking this course. She just wasn't sure that this was the kind of adjustment she wanted to make in her life. There were many other, apparently good recommendations:

Confusing Solutions

''What will I do?'' Ann asks, ''What will I do?''

Everyone seems to have a good reason for the suggestion they make. I just can't decide what to do.''

Ann felt herself unable to manage her situation. Indeed, she was not only unable to choose from among the courses suggested, but increasingly, she found herself ready to give up. Her survival instincts told her to drop everything or get rid of it all or walk away. Increasingly, Ann found herself in an all-or-nothing situation and favoring the latter course at that. She was less and less reasonable.

Confusing Reasons

Think about Ann for a moment. There were four recommendations that Ann considered. We assume that they won't all work for her, and that maybe only one course will work for her. That means that the other three do not work as well. If four people made four different recommendations, then three of them did not recommend what was best for Ann.

We may be making rather than solving problems. If Ann acts upon an inappropriate course of action and it does not resolve the problem, then she may be worse off than before. Not only did she waste valuable time and energy but also she is no closer to solving the problem.

Furthermore, she may have created new problems. For example, if she hired a babysitter or housekeeper, her children might have established a relationship with that person, either positive or negative, or mixed. If Ann had to end that relationship because her choice had been unproductive for her, new responsibilities might have been created.

Making Problems

If you recommended one of the courses for Ann, you are just like many of us. You listen for a while when people share problems. Then you recommend a course of action.

"What is wrong with that?" you might ask.

Nothing is wrong with it if it doesn't really matter to you if the course works or not.

Everything is wrong with it if you really care about what happens to the person who has a problem.

Trouble is, most of the courses recommended won't work for a given individual.

Compounding Problems

Attending to Sources of Information

The first and most important **PPS** skill is the interpersonal skill of attending to the sources of information about the problem. There are three sets of skills involved in attending. The first set of skills emphasizes attending physically to the basic sources of information. We do this by "squaring" with Ann, leaning toward her, and making eye contact with her. We attend physically so that we can observe Ann accurately. We observe the appearance and behavior of Ann. Finally, we attend and observe so that we can listen to Ann. We listen to both the words and the "music" behind the words, i.e., the content and the feeling expressed. We listen so that we can understand the meaning of this experience for her.

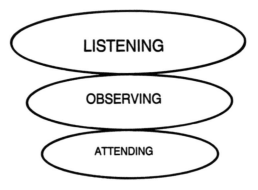

LISTENING

OBSERVING

ATTENDING

Attending

Attending to the sources of information does two things: 1) it involves these sources in the problem-solving process; and 2) it involves us, the helpers, in the problem-solving process. In attending to Ann, we involve her in sharing personal information that will help her to help herself. In the process, we become involved in the problem-solving process. We gather information by observing and listening. This information will help us to help Ann.

Attending ⟶ Involving

When we look at Ann physically, we are impressed by her size. She is physically large and apparently strong, suggesting good physical resources. She is attractive, although she carries a little more weight than is appropriate for her frame. However, Ann carries herself in a hunched manner, suggesting that she is trying to hide her strength. Her movements are slow and listless. She seems tired although there are some aspects of physical work which she enjoys when she is feeling well. In particular, keeping her own home in order has personal significance. We wonder how she can continue such an active schedule. We respond to her:

"You feel tired because there's just so much to do."

Observing Physically

We assess Ann emotionally. We interact with her. Her eyelids droop and she looks worn out. But there are moments of alertness and intensity, particularly when she summons her resolve to manage things, "to make them come out right," or when she speaks of her children and her great love for them. Her speech is monotoned and disjunctive except for these intense moments when it is rapid and lucid. She relates to us in a timid manner, suggesting years of conditioning instead of openness in an encounter. She is unable to respond accurately to our experience in the interaction. However, we can respond to her experience.

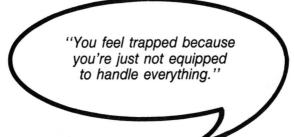

"You feel trapped because you're just not equipped to handle everything."

Observing Emotionally

Intellectually, Ann comes across as a bright person whose awareness has been dulled. While she is interested in the intellectual aspects of her teaching job and her graduate education, she relates a perspective of her world that does not include her own role. She functions mechanically, drawing upon her developed intellectual resources, rather than entering the moment creatively. She understands roles better than she does people. We reflect the feeling and meaning of her experience. Attending prepares us to respond to facilitate exploring.

Observing Intellectually

Exploring the Problem

We cannot develop a problem if we have not explored it. The second most critical interpersonal problem-solving skill is exploring. The person with the problem (helpee) must explore the problem thoroughly.

By exploration we mean an examination of all material that is relevant to the helpee's personal problems. This exploration will focus upon the specifics of the helpee's experience in relation to the problem. In particular, the exploration will focus upon the helpee's experience of herself as well as her experience of herself in relation to her world.

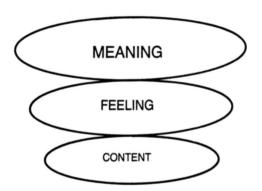

Exploring

In order to facilitate helpee exploration, we must respond accurately to the helpee's experience. Initially, we emphasize understanding the helpee's behavior in terms that can be verified or validated by others. Verbally, we emphasize responsiveness to the helpee at her level of expression. We respond to both the feeling and the meaning expressed by the helpee. We try to focus on how the helpee experiences herself. The material explored by the helpee will provide us with the material we need to understand the problem.

Responding ⟶ Exploring

In exploring herself, Ann isolates her feeling from her intellect, emphasizing the latter. She gives no evidence of emotional closeness to her experiences. She relates a life history of hard work and conditioned humility. She has been taught not to expect much from the world. What little she gets she has most certainly earned. And she is grateful! Life has been a real struggle for her, not because she did not have the resources, but because she has so many responsibilities. Now, she is struggling once again, not to free herself to emerge and grow but to return to "normalcy." We respond again to her:

"You feel frustrated because nothing seems to work out for you."

Responding to Content

We continue to respond to Ann in order to facilitate her exploration. Thus, we listen in an attempt to "hear" Ann's expressions. We respond in an attempt to help both helpee and helper understand accurately the breadth and depth of her expressions.

"Sometimes I just get so tired of everything. I just want to walk away from it all. Or, worse yet, end it all..."

"Sometimes you feel so desperate that you would consider the worst things just to have peace again."

Responding to Feeling

The meaning for Ann is the reason for the feeling. In exploring, we find that Ann experiences herself as being alone. No one shares her burdens. Not her husband! Not any of her friends! More important, she is alone in relation to her whole world. She is a person of superior talents who felt she had to settle for less in a world that has not provided a place for superior women. We respond to her experience. Responding prepares us for personalizing understanding.

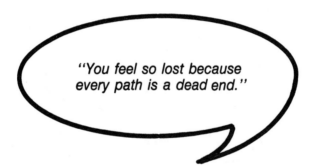

Responding to Meaning

Understanding the Problem

Exploration leads to understanding. By "understanding the problem," we mean understanding how the problem is relevant to the helpee's functioning. If we understand fully how the problem prevents him from functioning, then we may develop goals that will facilitate his functioning.

Again, we want to focus our understanding on how the helpee experiences himself in relation to his problem. We want to fully develop the picture of the helpee's feelings about himself. We want to emphasize the development of a picture of the helpee's feelings about himself in relation to his world. We want to understand how the particular problems involved fit into this picture.

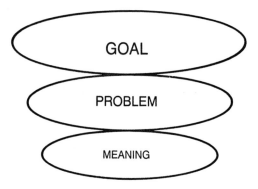

GOAL

PROBLEM

MEANING

Understanding

In order to facilitate the development of these pictures of self, we must also respond to the helpee at levels beyond what she has expressed. We must call upon our own experience in living. Clearly, we must have ourselves "together" to do this. To accomplish this with the helpee, we must first respond to each individual experience. Then we must utilize our own life experience to put the pieces of the helpee's experiences together in a complete picture. We put the whole picture together when we personalize the helpee's experience and facilitate the helpee's understanding.

Personalizing ⟶ Understanding

Because Ann feels that she has to earn her way every moment, she has struggled to secure a place for herself by her hard work. We must understand the personal implications of the assumptions Ann makes about herself. We must understand what there is about Ann that has contributed to the problems. It is not enough to explore Ann's experience of herself and her world. There are, to be sure, retarding forces in the world. We must also understand how Ann made herself vulnerable to that part of the world. We must search out those common themes about self that Ann is repeatedly expressing. We must personalize the meaning of these experiences in order to facilitate the understanding of personal implications.

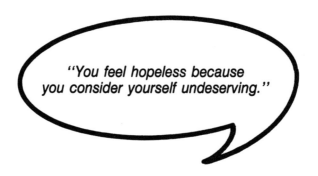

"You feel hopeless because you consider yourself undeserving."

Personalizing the Meaning

Ann has secured her place in the world by being the "work horse" for others less able than herself, including her husband. She has extended herself in a variety of activities, but she hasn't invested seriously in any of them. She has "spread herself thin" in her attempt to cover all bases, rather than involving herself deeply in any one set of activities that might provide real rewards for her. She has asked for and received nothing for herself. She is unable to free herself of bonds that she has helped to tie. In part, then, she has filled the hole with water in which she now feels to be drowning. We respond to her in a way that allows her to work with deeper understanding. We respond by personalizing her experience of her own deficits.

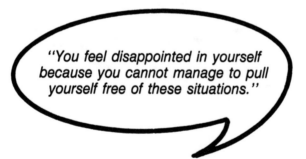

"You feel disappointed in yourself because you cannot manage to pull yourself free of these situations."

Personalizing the Problem

At the same time, Ann has not given up on herself. She continues to struggle to find a way to free herself. She finds hope in both the accuracy of your responses and the fact that you are willing to support her in facing her problems. In this respect she is eager to get started on her problem-solving mission. You respond to her changing experience by personalizing the goal.

"You feel eager to get started in learning to manage your life situations."

Personalizing the Goal

You may, if you wish, attempt to apply these understanding skills to your own problem or that of another learning with you. You may pair up or work in "training triads" with one person as helper, one as helpee, and one as "trainer." Conceive of a simple problem that you have. Apply the following understanding skills. This exercise should give you a good understanding of the goal.

Attending
1. Attend physically to the relevant sources of information about the person.

2. Index your observations of the appearance and behavior of the person in the following areas:
   a. Physical _____
   b. Emotional _____
   c. Intellectual _____

3. Listen to the experessions of the person in the following areas:
   a. Content _____
   b. Feeling _____
   c. Meaning _____

Responding
1. Respond to the content:
   "You said _____ ."

2. Respond to the feeling:
   "You feel _____ ."

3. Respond to the meaning:
   "You feel _____ because _____ ."

Personalizing
1. Personalize the meaning:
   "You feel _____ because you _____ ."

2. Personalize the problem:
   "You feel ___ because you cannot ___ ."

3. Personalize the goal:
   "You feel ____ because you cannot ____ and you really want to _____ ."

Applying Understanding Skills

In summary, we **attend** to involve, **respond** to explore, **personalize** to understand. All productive problem-solving requires personal processing. In processing, we transform data into personally meaningful information. The interpersonal skills used with Ann are the same that we must use with all persons with problems. Understanding the problem helps us to be more productive in our problem-solving efforts. Understanding the problem prepares us for analyzing the problem.

Productive Understanding Skills

3
ANALYZING
THE PROBLEM

John had a problem relating to people. At home, at school and at work, he seemed to elicit negative reactions from people. He really was unhappy with the results. He did not want to have his feelings hurt all of the time. Nor did he want to hurt other people's feelings. He sought help: how could he learn to relate to people in such a way as to elicit positive reactions from them? In order to answer this question, he first had to analyze the problem and then use the same dimensions to synthesize a goal.

SYNTHESIZING GOALS

ANALYZING PROBLEMS

Analyzing

Analyzing the Problem

Analyzing the problem means breaking the problem down into its component parts. The component parts emphasize the operational dimensions of the problem: components, functions, processes, conditions, standards. The operational dimensions of the problem answer the basic interrogatives about the problem: who, what, why, how, when and where?

Problem Analysis:	Questions:
Components	— *Who* and *what* is involved?
Functions	— *What* are they doing?
Processes	— *Why* and *how* are they doing it?
Conditions	— *Where* and *when* are they doing it?
Standards	— *How well* are they doing it?

The helper involved John in exploring and understanding his problem. Together, they found that John had developed a self-defeating lifestyle. In order to protect himself from the hurt that he had experienced from others earlier in his life, he did not relate to people. He was inattentive in his posturing and negative in his verbalizations. In turn, he was hurt by the negative reactions of others. Now he expressed disappointment in his behavior: "I feel disappointed in myself because I cannot relate constructively and I really want to." Together, the helper and John analyzed the operational dimensions of John's problem.

Problem Analysis:

Components	—	John
Functions	—	relates to people
Processes	—	by not attending and by criticizing others so that he won't get hurt
Conditions	—	at home on his schedule
Standards	—	to the point of eliciting negative reactions

Analyzing Operational Dimensions

In a similar manner, Ann's self-defeating behavior may be analyzed. Because she feels that she must earn her way every moment of her life, Ann takes on more responsibilities than she can manage. Consequently, because she is overwhelmed, she does not earn her way in *any* moment of her life.

Problem Analysis:

Components	—	Ann
Functions	—	assumes responsibilities
Processes	—	by over-extending herself so that she can satisfy everyone
Conditions	—	at home, school and work
Standards	—	to the point where she fails to discharge any responsibilities

Analyzing Problem Components

While many problems do not initally appear to require extensive problem analyses, it is nevertheless helpful to analyze the operational dimensions. For example, the discrepancy between a limited personal repertoire of responses and an extensive required repertoire of responses may be formulated as follows:

Limited Personal Responses $<$ **Required extensive responses**

This equation may be further analyzed in terms of the discrepancy between the quantity (Qu) and quality (Ql) of operational dimensions:

Personal Responses	$<$	Required Responses
Limited **Qu** +/or **Ql** of **Components**		Extensive **Qu** +/or **Ql** of **Components**
Limited **Qu** +/or **Ql** of **Functions**		Extensive **Qu** +/or **Ql** of **Functions**
Limited **Qu** +/or **Ql** of **Processes**		Extensive **Qu** +/or **Ql** of **Processes**
Limited **Qu** +/or **Ql** of **Conditions**		Extensive **Qu** +/or **Ql** of **Conditions**
Limited **Qu** +/or **Ql** of **Standards**		Extensive **Qu** +/or **Ql** of **Standards**

Comparing Problem Analyses

Other problems do not seem to require an extensive problem analyses. Deciding between two or more apparently equally attractive or unattractive opportunities may be stated as follows:

Opportunity #1 = Opportunity #2

A decision analysis of the dimensions may reveal more precise differences than were originally seen:

Opportunity #1 Dimensions	=	Opportunity #2 Dimensions
Components #1	=	Components #2
Functions #1	<	Functions #2
Processes #1	>	Processes #2
Conditions #1	=	Conditions #2
Standards #1	=	Standards #2

In this case, the functions and processes of an apparently equal opportunity are unequal. Any one or more of the dimensions may be equal or unequal.

Comparing Decision Analyses

Synthesizing the Goal

Analyzing the problem prepares us for synthesizing the goal. In a very real sense, the goal is simply the other side of the problem. Where there are deficits, assets may be generated as goals. Where there are realities, expectations or intentions may be generated as goals. We apply the same operational dimensions in synthesizing the goal that we applied in analyzing the problem.

Goal Synthesis:		Questions:
Components	—	*Who* and *what* do we expect to be involved?
Functions	—	*What* do we expect them to do?
Processes	—	*Why* and *how* do we expect them to do it?
Conditions	—	*Where* and *when* do we expect them to do it?
Standards	—	*How well* do we expect them to do it?

Thus, for example, in the case of John's self-defeating interpersonal behavior, we may generate goals by synthesizing the expected operational dimensions involved:

Goal Synthesis:

Components	—	The "new John"
Functions	—	will relate to "new people"
Processes	—	by attending and responding so that he can facilitate others
Conditions	—	everywhere and at all times
Standards	—	at the level of eliciting reciprocal affect

In this case, all of the operational dimensions were reversed to define a goal of producing a "new John" who can relate productively to people.

Synthesizing Operational Dimensions

In a similar manner, Ann's self-generating goals may be synthesized in operational dimensions:

Goal Synthesis:

Components	—	Ann
Functions	—	will assume responsibilities
Processes	—	by making cost-beneficial decisions so that she can be productive
Conditions	—	at home, school and work
Standards	—	at the level where she can handle all of her responsibilities at highly productive levels

In this case, Ann changes only the processes (*how* and *why*) and the standards (*how well*) in synthesizing her new goal.

Synthesizing Problem Components

In a like manner, we can synthesize the goal in comparative problem analysis. We can simply assume as our goals either the quantitative or qualitative dimensions of one or more of the required operational dimensions. For example, quantitatively (**Qu**), we may look to increase either the volume, rate or timeliness of one or more of the dimensions of our responses. In turn, qualitatively (**Ql**), we may expect to increase either the functionality, accuracy or creativity of one or more of the dimensions of our responses.

Response Goals:

Defined **Qu** +/or **Ql** of **Components**
Defined **Qu** +/or **Ql** of **Functions**
Defined **Qu** +/or **Ql** of **Processes**
Defined **Qu** +/or **Ql** of **Conditions**
Defined **Qu** +/or **Ql** of **Standards**

In this case, we may define as response goals one or more of the quantitative or qualitative factors of the operational dimensions.

Comparing Goal Syntheses

In turn, in making decisions, we may generate a similar decision synthesis. Thus, where we may have analyzed the problem as equality of opportunity, we may now synthesize the decision as inequality of opportunity.

Opportunity #1 Dimensions	=	Opportunity #2 Dimensions
Components #1	> or <	Components #2
Functions #1	> or <	Functions #2
Processes #1	> or <	Processes #2
Conditions #1	> or <	Conditions #2
Standards #1	> or <	Standards #2

In this case, we look to make the operational dimensions greater than (>) or less than (<) the corresponding dimensions of other opportunities. In the case of a problem analysis of unequality (≠), we may wish to make the opportunities (=).

Comparing Decision Syntheses

You may wish to apply your problem analyzing skills. You may practice this in pairs or in "training triads." Simply analyze a simple problem in terms of its operational dimensions. Then synthesize the goals in terms of their operational dimensions. In synthesizing the goals, you may change one or more of the operational dimensions. Your synthesized goal becomes the objective of your problem-solving efforts.

Problem: Goal:

Components
(WHO and WHAT?)

Functions
(WHAT?)

Processes
(WHY and HOW?)

Conditions
(WHERE and WHEN?)

Standards
(HOW WELL?)

Applying Analyzing Skills

In summary, problems may be analyzed and goals synthesized using operational dimensions: components, functions, processes, conditions, standards. The creative application and transfer of these dimensions will enable us to analyze any phenomenon and synthesize any goal for that phenomenon. Any problem that can be conceived of can be analyzed. Any problem that can be analyzed can be synthesized in a goal. Any goal that can be synthesized can be achieved. Our **PPS** skills will enable us to achieve any goals.

4
EXPANDING
ALTERNATIVE
COURSES

Susan had a problem in choosing between going to college or not. She had all the credentials which she needed to qualify. However, she was not sure that she could endure four more years of academic work. She found the possibility of "hands-on" work experiences attractive. Susan clearly had two alternative courses of action: to go to college; to not go to college and to work. These two courses of action exist for nearly all problems. They may be labeled the "Go/No Go" courses. Indeed, most people attempt to resolve most of their problems by choosing one of these courses. That is why most peole fail to resolve their problems most of the time. There are a variety of ways of generating alternative courses of action in between these extremes. These involve people, program and organizational alternatives.

Expanding

Nevertheless, "Go/No Go" courses are fundamental to the development of alternative courses of action. These courses represent the extreme options: "Either I will do it or I won't!"; "Either I will stay or I will leave!" They do, indeed, represent viable alternatives. Sometimes it is necessary to make extreme choices. But choices this extreme are not often necessary. Most often, we may anchor our alternatives like bookends at both ends of a line with the "Go/No Go" choices. In between, we will expand the alternatives to the extreme courses. For example, in between Susan's "Go/Don't Go" to college choices lie a number of other alternatives:

1. Seek career counseling assistance
2. Receive a tutorial experience
3. Enroll in career placing program
4. Create an internship program
5. Organize a cultural experience
6. Formalize a work/study experience

These are only a sample of the courses available to Susan as alternatives to the two "Go/No Go" choices. We may organize these alternatives as follows:

"GO" EXTREME						"NO GO" EXTREME
Go to College	Tutorial Experiences	Career Counseling	Intern Program	Cultural Experience	Work/ Study	Don't go to College

"Go/No Go" Courses

People Alternatives

One of the helpful ways of expanding alternatives is to generate "People Alternatives." People alternatives are courses of action oriented around specific people or specific personal services. For example, Susan's first two alternatives were centered around people: the first and most obvious being to seek career counseling assistance from a personal career counselor; the second alternative being to receive some kind of personal tutorial experience preliminary to making a career choice. People alternatives provide us a way of generating alternative courses based upon personal contact. For example, in seeking to place a "drop out" or delinquent, we may first think of people specially equipped to manage such an experience. Similarly, in our own educational or career experiences, we may think of people with expertise who are equipped to provide mentoring experiences.

In a similar manner, Ann can organize her different courses of action around "people" alternatives. For example, two of the recommendations she received emphasized people alternatives.

PEOPLE ALTERNATIVES

"GO" EXTREME			"NO GO" EXTREME
Continuing Everything	Getting Babysitter	Getting Housekeeper	Quitting Everything

Getting a babysitter or getting a housekeeper are people alternatives organized around contracts for personal services. What are some other people alternatives you can think of? Simply consider the different functions Ann attempts and generate options built around people and the services they provide.

Expanding People Alternatives

In the case of John's self-defeating interpersonal behavior, we may anchor the alternatives between the two extremes of becoming involved and not becoming involved with people. Within the option of becoming involved, we may generate several people alternative courses of action:

PEOPLE ALTERNATIVES

"GO" EXTREME				"NO GO" EXTREME
Continuing Everything	Counseling Experience	Modeling Relationship	Mentoring Relationship	Not Becoming Involved

In this instance, we have generated several alternative people courses of action: becoming involved in a counseling experience where John can develop a new and more productive set of assumptions about his world; becoming involved in a modeling relationship where John can model his behavior after a successful person; becoming involved in a mentoring relationship where John can be guided in his development. What are some other people alternatives that you can think of?

Developing People Courses

Program Alternatives

A second helpful way of expanding alternatives is to generate "program alternatives." Program alternatives are courses of action oriented around specific programs that may be helpful in resolving the problem. For example, Susan's third and fourth alternatives were generated by program alternatives: enrolling in a career planning program; and creating an internship program. Program alternatives provide a way of generating alternative courses based upon specific programs. For example, there may be specific training or experiential programs in living, learning or working areas that have the potential of resolving problems.

Similarly, Ann can generate program alternatives that were not originally recommended.

PROGRAM ALTERNATIVES

"GO" EXTREME			"NO GO" EXTREME
Continuing Everything	Time Management	Performance Planning	Quitting Everything

Enrolling in a time management or a performance planning training program might help resolve some of Ann's problems. What are some other program alternatives you can think of? Again, consider the different functions Ann attempts and generate options built around programs and the services they provide.

Expanding Program Alternatives

In John's case, we may generate several program alternatives.

PROGRAM ALTERNATIVES

"GO" EXTREME				"NO GO" EXTREME
Continuing Everything	IPS Training	Self-Control Programs	Conditioning Programs	Not Becoming Involved

In this instance, we have generated several alternative program courses: receiving interpersonal processing skills (IPS) training; receiving training in self-control; receiving conditioning programs that will facilitate self-control. What are some other program alternatives that you can think of?

Developing Program Courses

Organization Alternatives

Finally, organizing or reorganizing is a helpful way of expanding alternatives. "Organizing alternatives" are oriented around configuring or reconfiguring different people and program commitments. For example, Susan's fifth and sixth recommendations were generated by organization alternatives: becoming involved in a cultural experience that delayed decision-making; and organizing a work/study program. Organization alternatives provide us a way of generating alternative courses based upon the organization and reorganization of priorities. For example, we may eliminate or add, partially or completely, any aspect of people or program commitments in our jobs, our education, and our lives.

Similarly, Ann may note the organization alternatives that were part of her original recommendations.

ORGANIZATION ALTERNATIVES

"GO" EXTREME			"NO GO" EXTREME
Continuing Everything	Quit Job	Quit School	Quitting Everything

Quitting her job and quitting school were two of the recommended organization alternatives. What are some other organization alternatives? Consider the different functions Ann attempts and reorganize their priorities.

Expanding Organization Alternatives

In John's case, we may generate several organization alternatives.

ORGANIZATION ALTERNATIVES

"GO" EXTREME				"NO GO" EXTREME
Continuing Everything	Reorganize Relations	Reorganize Contracts	Reorganize Contracts	Not Becoming Involved

In this instance, we have generated several alternative organization courses: reorganizing the intensity of the different relationships; reorganizing the frequency of contacts; reorganizing the nature of the contracts in the different relationships. What are some other organization alternatives that you can think of?

Developing Organization Courses

You may wish to apply your alternative expanding skills. Again, you may practice alone, in pairs or in "training triads." Simply generate people, program and organization alternatives for a straightforward problem of your own choosing. You will consider how these alternatives impact upon your values.

ALTERNATIVE COURSES OF ACTION

"GO" EXTREME	PEOPLE ALTERNATIVES	PROGRAM ALTERNATIVES	ORGANIZATION ALTERNATIVES	"NO GO" EXTREME
_____	_____	_____	_____	_____
_____	_____	_____	_____	_____
_____	_____	_____	_____	_____
_____	_____	_____	_____	_____
_____	_____	_____	_____	_____

Applying Expanding Skills

In summary, alternative courses of action may be generated between the "Go" and "No Go" extremes: people, program and organization alternatives. We will now determine which of these alternatives or combination of alternatives will best satisfy our values. Hopefully, we will find that combination of alternatives that helps us to be most productive. There are alternatives in every crises, and solutions to every problem. We must now consider the costs and benefits of these solutions.

Productive Expanding Skills

5
DEFINING
VALUES

Bill always believed that his values constituted the core of his integrity. They had guided him in his decision-making throughout his life. Yet he never felt that his values were fully satisfied. Perhaps this was because he focused upon the benefits which he hoped to achieve in his life. The benefits are only one part of the values equation. People also need to come to terms with the investments of resources which they are willing to make to achieve the benefits. Perhaps most important, they must be able to define their values in such a manner that they can determine whether or not they have achieved them.

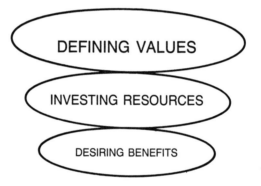

Defining

Desiring Benefits

Values are the meanings we attach to people, data or things. Values are the things that matter to us. Values reflect our own most personal experiences. No two people in the world share precisely the same values. The problem is defining the values to reflect one's personal experience. Usually when we consider values, we are considering the benefits we hope to accrue in life. For example, Bill's values centered around his home and his family. His life was oriented toward making his home secure and comfortable and facilitating the future development of his children. We may term these living or life benefits. Other benefits include learning and working benefits. The benefits we desire guide the efforts we make in life.

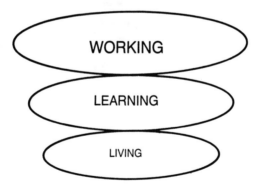

Desiring Benefits

Living benefits, like Bill's primary values, emphasize home and family values. Usually they revolve around the traditional family, but for some people the family extends beyond relatives. Infrequently, people relate to the community-at-large as part of their family.

One of Ann's values revolved around her role as homemaker for four children and a spouse. Similarly, one of John's values emphasized relating at home with his parents and siblings. These values direct people's efforts toward achieving living benefits.

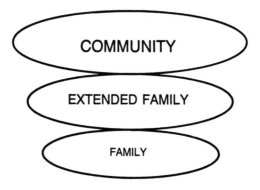

Desiring Living Benefits

Learning benefits tend to emphasize the benefits from education, training and mentoring experiences. Usually, they revolve around advancements in professional expertise. For example, Ann was attempting to advance herself professionally in her graduate studies. John needed to learn to relate interpersonally with teachers and peers at school. Susan was trying to figure out what she wanted in her learning values. These values direct people's efforts toward achieving learning benefits.

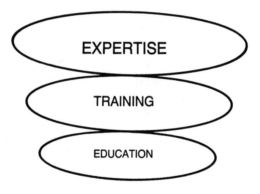

Desiring Learning Benefits

Working benefits tend to emphasize our benefits from vocations or avocations. Defining careers as the way we live our lives, we may consider working benefits to include anything that we derive from our vocational or avocational efforts. For some people, the benefits revolve around personal benefits like job security and working conditions, salary and freedom. These were the values that John and Susan were exploring. For other people, the benefits are oriented toward others, in the sense that they are concerned about quantity and quality of the products they produce, the services they provide and the benefits that consumers derive from their products and services. For example, Ann was a serious teacher who sought not only working benefits for herself as well as learning benefits for her students through the skills she used and the knowledge she offered. These values direct people's efforts toward achieving learning benefits.

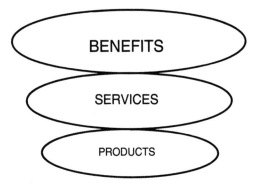

Desiring Working Benefits

Investing Resources

The other part of values has to do with the resources we are willing to invest in order to achieve the desired benefits. These resources revolve around our physical, emotional and intellectual resources. For example, in order to achieve his living benefits, Bill was willing to invest his physical energies and intellectual skills. The resources we are willing to invest determine the benefits we are able to achieve.

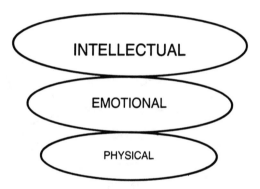

Physical resources include our investment of physical energies and efforts. They emphasize the physical labor we need to perform tasks. As well, physical resources emphasize the diet, rest and exercise that we invest in order to develop and maintain our physical energies. For example, Ann had overextended herself in investing physical resources: she simply did not have the energy to continue her level of investment. Bill, on the other hand, was young and vigorous and not overextended: he had plentiful physical energies he could invest in achieving his home and family benefits. These are the physical resource investments that determine the level of benefits we can achieve.

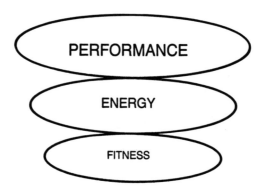

Investing Physical Resources

Emotional resources include our investment of personal motivation, and intrapersonal and interpersonal relations. How we feel about ourselves intrapersonally determines the levels of motivation we invest in our worlds and the level of interpersonal relations with which we relate to the people in our worlds. These resources determine the way we relate to ourselves, our worlds and the people in it. For example, Ann was exhausted motivationally, intrapersonally and interpersonally. John was motivated, but suffered interpersonally because of the way he felt about himself intrapersonally. These are the emotional resource investments which determine the level of benefits we can achieve.

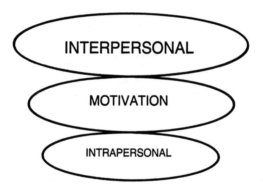

Investing Emotional Resources

Intellectual resources include our investment of personal skills, knowledge and responses. They emphasize our ways of perceiving, organizing, intervening in and impacting our worlds cognitively. For example, Ann was skilled intellectually. John behaved exclusively as a critic. Bill was committed to knowing everything he needed to know in order to achieve his living benefits. These are the intellectual resource investments that determine the level of benefits we can achieve.

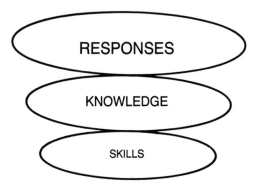

Investing Intellectual Resources

Defining Values

It is not enough to have specified our values. We must also define our values in terms that are observable and measurable. That way we will know when, if, and at what level we have achieved our values. For example, if we define an acceptable salary level at $20,000, then we can tell whether we have achieved it or not. Similarly, if we define a desirable interpersonal value as sharing experiences with others once every day, then we can measure its achievement. It is the same with learning one new skill per week as an intellectual value. Defining values emphasizes defining levels of favorability, levels of productivity and, finally, levels of achievement.

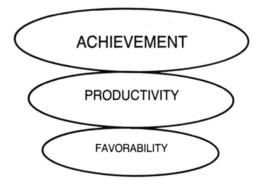

Defining Favorability Levels

We can define our values in terms of their various levels of favorability of us. Thus "+ +" represents high levels of favorability. Similarly, " − −" represents highly unfavorable levels of our values. Other values range inbetween these extremes. Favorable is "+" or positive. Acceptable is "0" or neutral or minimal. Unfavorable is " −" or negative. These levels of values can be defined in numbers. The most useful numbers have to do with time: the amount of time, the number of times, the percentage of time. Time may also be translated into money in terms of the value of the time.

Levels of Favorability:

Highly Favorable	—	+ +
Favorable	—	+
Acceptable	—	0
Unfavorable	—	−
Highly Unfavorable	—	− −

For example, we may define Bill's salary values which can be transformed into his home and family living benefits. At the most favorable level, Bill desires a salary of $25,000 or greater. At the most unfavorable level, Bill rejects a salary of less than $10,000. A salary in the range of $15,000—$19,000 is acceptable.

SALARY BENEFITS:

+ +	—	>	$25,000		
	—		$20,000	–	$24,000
0	—		$15,000	–	$19,000
–	—		$10,000	–	$14,000
– –	—	<	$10,000		

Defining Living Benefits

Susan's learning benefits may be defined in terms of the number of skills she learns over a period of time. Thus, at the highly favorable level, she learns one skill per week, while at the least favorable level, she learns less than one skill per two months. One skill per month is acceptable.

SKILLS BENEFITS:

+ +	—	1 Skill per week
+	—	1 Skill per 2 weeks
0	—	1 Skill per month
−	—	1 Skill per 2 months
− −	—	< 1 Skill per 2 months

Defining Learning Benefits

In turn, John's interpersonal performance benefits may be defined in terms of maximizing the results outputs and minimizing the resource inputs in his interpersonal efforts.

PERFORMANCE BENEFITS:

+ +   —   Maximimum Results Outputs (RO) and
            Minimum Resource Inputs (RI)

  +   —   Maximum Results Outputs (RO) or
            Minimum Resource Inputs (RI)

  0   —   Same Outputs (O) and Inputs (I)

  −   —   Minimum Results Outputs (RO) or
            Maximum Results Inputs (RI)

− −   —   Minimum Results Outputs (RO) and
            Maximum Results Inputs (RI)

Defining Working Benefits

We may define Ann's working benefits in terms of her consumers' benefits. A conscientious teacher, Ann desires 90%-100% of her learners to be performing at grade level by the end of the academic year. Less than 60% is highly unfavorable and 70-79% is acceptable. In a very real sense, the favorability scale is Ann's own report card for her performance as a teacher.

ACHIEVEMENT BENEFITS:

```
+ +   —   90 - 100% learners at grade level for year
  +   —   80 -  89% learners at grade level for year
  0   —   70 -  79% learners at grade level for year
  –   —   60 -  69% learners at grade level for year
– –   —   <    60% learners at grade level for year
```

Defining Working Benefits

Just as we define benefits, so may we define investments. For example, we may define Bill's willingness to
work long hours in order to achieve his salary benefits.
At the most favorable levels, Bill is willing to work 60
hours or more per week. At the least favorable levels, he
is willing to work 30 or less hours per week. At acceptable levels, he is willing to work 40-49 hours per week.

TIME INVESTMENTS:

    + +   —   > 60 hours per week
      +   —   50-59 hours per week
      0   —   40-49 hours per week
      –   —   30-39 hours per week
    – –   —   < 30 hours per week

Defining Physical Investments

John, on the other hand, was trying to minimize his time investments in interpersonal relations. In other words, he wanted to maximize his efficiency and effectiveness at the same time.

TIME PER PERSON:

+ +	—	< 5	minutes
+	—	5- 6	minutes
0	—	7- 8	minutes
–	—	9-10	minutes
– –	—	> 10	minutes

Defining Physical Investments

Similarly, Susan's emotional investments may be defined as the amount of time she is motivated about what she is doing. At the most favorable levels, she finds herself motivated 90%-100% of the time. At the least favorable levels, she is motivated less than 60% of the time. Being motivated 70%-79% of the time is acceptable.

MOTIVATION INVESTMENTS:

+ +	—	90% -	100% of the time
+	—	80% -	89% of the time
0	—	70% -	79% of the time
–	—	60% -	69% of the time
– –	—	<	60% of the time

Defining Emotional Investments

In the same manner, we may define Ann's intellectual investment in accomplishing her student achievement benefits. She is willing to create one creative transfer product of the skills applications she is teaching: every week (+ +); every two weeks (+); every month (0); every two months (−); less than every two months (− −).

TRANSFER INVESTMENT:

+ +	—	1 creative product per week
+	—	1 creative product per 2 weeks
0	—	1 creative product per month
−	—	1 creative product per 2 months
− −	— <	1 creative product per 2 months

Defining Intellectual Investments

Defining Productivity Levels

When we define the benefits and the investments in tandem, we may define levels of productivity. When we seek to increase benefits while simultaneously reducing investment, we are defining productivity. Thus benefits are maximum while investments are minimum.

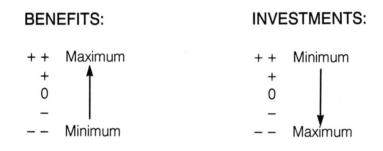

BENEFITS:		INVESTMENTS:	
+ +	Maximum	+ +	Minimum
+		+	
0		0	
−		−	
− −	Minimum	− −	Maximum

John has already built productivity values into his interpersonal perfomance values. As can be seen, he is attempting to maximize his benefits while minimizing his investments.

PERFORMANCE BENEFITS: TIME INVESTMENTS:

+ +	—	Max. RO	+ Min. RI
+	—	Max. RO	or Min. RI
0	—	Same RO	+ RI
–	—	Min. RO	or Max. RI
– –	—	Min. RO	+ Max. RI

+ +	—	< 5 min.
+	—	5-6 min.
0	—	7-8 min.
–	—	9-10 min.
– –	—	> 10 min.

Relating Costs and Benefits

On the other hand, Bill would be increasing the productivity levels of his values if he simultaneously increased his salary while reducing the number of hours he worked. As can be seen, Bill upgrades his salary benefits while reversing his time investments. Bill is productive when he invests the minimum number of hours and achieves the maximum benefits.

SALARY BENEFITS:				TIME INVESTMENTS:			
+ +		—	> $30,000	+ +		—	< 30 hours
	+	—	$25,000-29,000		+	—	30-39 hours
	0	—	$20,000-24,000			—	40-49 hours
	—	—	$15,000-19,000		—	—	50-59 hours
— —		—	< $15,000	— —		—	> 60 hours

Relating Costs and Living Benefits

Similarly, Susan may achieve productivity by simultaneously reversing her motivation investments while improving her skill benefits. This means she will be more selective about investing herself. She can do this by being more mechanical in her other efforts where it is appropriate.

SKILL BENEFITS:

+ +	—	1 skill per day
+	—	1 skill per 2 days
0	—	1 skill per week
–	—	1 skill per 2 weeks
– –	—	< 1 skill per 2 weeks

MOTIVATION INVESTMENTS:

+ +	—	< 60% of time
+	—	60- 69% of time
0	—	70- 79% of time
–	—	80- 89% of time
– –	—	90-100% of time

Relating Costs and Learning Benefits

Likewise, Ann may achieve productivity by reversing her transfer investments and upgrading her achievement benefits. She can do this by teaching the learners to create the transfer products.

ACHIEVEMENT BENEFITS:

+ +	—	100% learners
+	—	95% learners
0	—	90% learners
–	—	80% learners
– –	—	< 80% learners

TRANSFER INVESTMENT:

+ +	—	No creative products per year
+	—	1 creative product per year
0	—	1 creative product per ½ year
–	—	1 creative product per month
– –	—	> 1 creative product per month

Relating Costs and Working Benefits

You may wish to apply your values defining skills to a problem you have chosen to work on. Select the appropriate benefits and investment values. Define them in terms of favorability levels. See if you can relate some of them to achieve productivity levels.

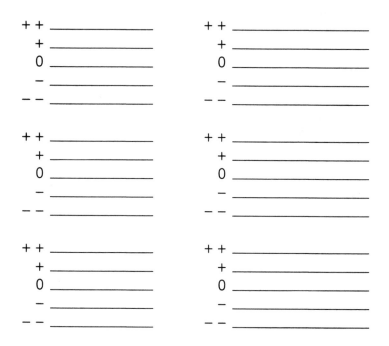

BENEFIT VALUES:

INVESTMENT VALUES:

++ _____
+ _____
0 _____
– _____
– – _____

++ _____
+ _____
0 _____
– _____
– – _____

++ _____
+ _____
0 _____
– _____
– – _____

++ _____
+ _____
0 _____
– _____
– – _____

++ _____
+ _____
0 _____
– _____
– – _____

++ _____
+ _____
0 _____
– _____
– – _____

Applying Defining Skills

In summary, values may be specified and defined in terms of favorability and/or productivity levels. We can now study the impact of the alternative courses of action upon these values in observable and measurable terms. Any value can be defined in quantitative or qualitative terms. Every value can, therefore, influence the direction of our problem-solving process.

Productive Values Skills

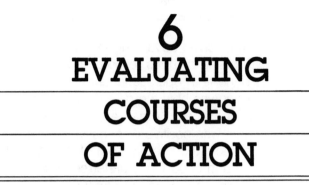

6
EVALUATING
COURSES
OF ACTION

Tom's problem involved advancing in his job. He understood how to define both his resource investments and his results benefits in operational terms. What he could not figure out was how the different courses of action impacted those values. He had a general notion of whether the impact was positive or negative. However, he was not sure about the specific level of impact and how it all added up in choosing a preferred course of action. To know this, Tom needed to know how to weight or prioritize his values and evaluate the impact of the various courses upon the values before adding up the total impact in choosing preferred courses.

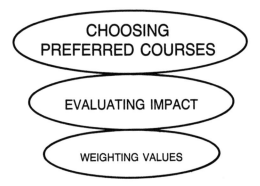

Evaluating Courses

Weighting Values

Weighting values prioritizes them in relation to each other. In other words, we may compare the relative importance of each value. One way to do this is to weight them from "1" to "10" in order of their importance. We can weight the most important value at "10" and the least important value at "1." The values inbetween may be weighted according to their relative importance by developing a hierarchy of values.

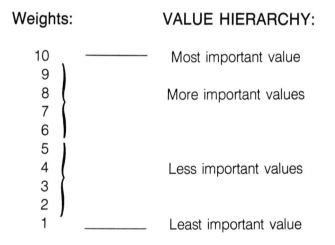

Weights:	VALUE HIERARCHY:
10 ———	Most important value
9	
8	More important values
7	
6	
5	
4	Less important values
3	
2	
1 ————	Least important value

For example, John had an overriding concern for interpersonal productivity that maximized the weight of performance and minimized the weight of time investments.

VALUE HIERARCHY:	Weights:
Interpersonal Performance	10
Time Investments	1

Weighting Benefits

In turn, Bill developed his value hierarchy and weighted his individual values. They reflect his overriding concern with salary increments that would lead to home and family benefits.

VALUE HIERARCHY:	Weights:
Home and Family	10
Salary	8
Time Investments	1

Weighting Benefits

Susan developed her value hierarchy for deciding between college and work. Her values reflected her domi-
nant concern for investing intellectually in learning skills.

VALUE HIERARCHY:	Weights:
Skill Benefits	10
Intellectual Investments	9
Enjoyment Investments	5
Motivation Investments	3

Weighting Investments

Finally, Ann developed a value hierarchy and weighted her individual values. They reflected her commitment to living, learning and working benefits as well as her willingness to invest resources to achieve these benefits.

VALUE HIERARCHY:	Weights:
Children Benefits	10
Husband Benefits	9
Professional Benefits	8
Student Benefits	7
Professional Investments	5
Home Investments	4
Educational Investments	3
Financial Investments	1

Weighting Investments and Benefits

Evaluating Impact

Evaluating the impact of the courses of action upon the values emphasizes studying the effects or potential effects of each course upon each step. Each course may have a range of impacts upon the value involved: highly favorable, favorable, acceptable, unfavorable, highly unfavorable. Given that the values are defined in terms of these favorability levels, assessing the impact of the courses involves estimating the level of favorability to be achieved by each course.

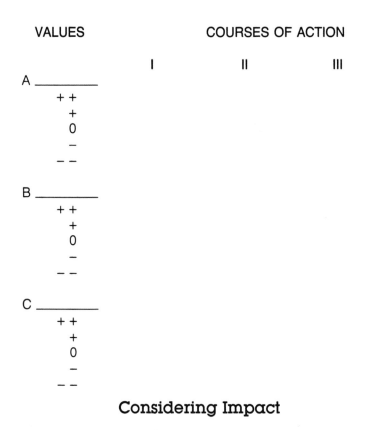

VALUES COURSES OF ACTION

I II III

A _____
+ +
+
0
–
– –

B _____
+ +
+
0
–
– –

C _____
+ +
+
0
–
– –

Considering Impact

For example, Tom finally determined that he had one overriding value for job advancement. This value he characterized as job productivity. He wanted to function in a job where he could maximize his productivity, i.e., maximize his results output while minimizing his resource input. He evaluated his alternative courses of action and found that in his scheduled promotion he would not be as productive as in his current job. A new job that he had been looking at held the most promise.

		COURSES OF ACTION		
		I	II	III
VALUE	(Weight)	Current Job	Scheduled Promotion	Job Change
Productivity	(10)			
+ + Productivity				+ +
+ Effectiveness/ Efficiency		+		
0 Maintenance			0	
− Ineffectiveness/ Inefficiency				
− − Non-Productivity				

Evaluating Courses

In a similar manner, Bill evaluated the courses of action available to him. As can be seen, Bill found that while overtime work promised a greater salary, preparing himself for job advancement held the most potential. On the other hand, it also would require the greatest investment of time. However, Bill did not weight the time investments heavily.

COURSES OF ACTION

VALUES	(Weight)	I Current Job	II Overtime Work	III Job Advancement
Salary	(10)			
+ + > 30K				+ +
+ 25-29K			+	
0 20-24K		0		
− 15K-19K				
− − < 15K				
Time	(1)			
+ + < 30 hours				
+ 30-39 hours				
0 40-49 hours		0		
− 50-59 hours		−		
− − > 60 hours				− −

Evaluating Impact

Likewise, John assessed the courses of action available to him to satisfy his value of improving his interpersonal performance and productivity. As can be seen, the interpersonal processing skills (IPS) program bearing most directly upon his values emerged as the most potent course of action.

COURSES OF ACTION

VALUES	(Wts)	I Counsel	II Model	III Mentor	IV IPS Training	V Self-Control	VI Cond. Prog.	VII Reorg. Relat.	VIII Reorg. Contacts	IX Reorg. Contracts
Interpersonal Performance	(10)									
++ RO+ & RI+					++					
+ RO+ or RI+		+	+	+		+	+	+	+	+
0 SAME										
– RO– or RI–										
– – RO– & RI–										
Time	(1)									
++ < 5 min.					++					
+ 5- 6 min.			+	+		+	+			
0 7- 8 min.		0						0	0	0
– 9-10 min.										
– – > 10 min.										

Evaluating Impact Upon Values

Susan evaluated the impact of the courses of action available to her. She found work/study, internship and tutorial experiences most positive. Remember, Susan defined her values from her frame of reference. They reflect the personal meaning she attaches to things. Consequently, the evaluations of the courses of action are personalized to her particular frame of reference.

COURSES OF ACTION

VALUES	(Wts)	I Tutorial	II Counseling	III Career Planning	IV Intern	V Culture	VI Work/Study
Skills	(10)	+	0	0	+ +	0	+ +
Intellect	(9)	+	0	0	+	0	+ +
Enjoyment	(5)	+	+	+	+	+ +	+ +
Motivation	(3)	+	+	+	+ +	0	+ +

Evaluating Course Impact

Ann also evaluated multiple courses of action using her extensive value hierarchy. As can be seen, continuing or quitting her current course are among the least favorable options in terms of their impact upon her values. Again, these are Ann's personalized evaluations of the impact of her courses of action upon her defined values.

COURSES OF ACTION

VALUES	(Wts)	I Continue Everything	II Babysitter	III Houjsekeeper	IV Time Training	V Perf. Planning	VI Quit Job	VII Quit School	VIII Quit Everything
Children	(10)	– –	– –	+ +	+	+	+ +	+	+ +
Husband	(9)	– –	+	+ +	+	+	+ +	+	+ +
Professional	(8)	– –	+	+	+	+	– –	0	– –
Students	(7)	– –	+	+	+	+	0	– –	– –
Prof. Invest.	(5)	– –	+	+	+	+	– –	+	– –
Home Invest.	(4)	– –	–	–	+	+	+	+	– –
Educ. Invest.	(3)	– –	+	+	+	+	+	– –	– –
Finc. Invest.	(1)	– –	–	–	0	0	– –	0	– –

Evaluating Course Potential

Choosing Preferred Courses

Choosing preferred courses of action is a mechanical process. Preferred courses of action are those courses which impact values most favorably. Preferred courses are chosen by: 1) multiplying the weights of the values by the impact of the courses; 2) sum-totaling the columns of weighted impact totals. The preferred course (*) will be that course with the highest column total.

COURSES OF ACTION

VALUES	(Weights)	I	II	III
A _____	(10)			
+ +				+ +(+20)
+			+(+10)	
0		0(0)		
−				
− −				
B _____	(5)			
+ +				
+		+(+5)		
0			0(0)	
−				−(− 5)
− −				
C _____	(1)			
+ +				+ +(+ 2)
+			+(+1)	
0		0(0)		
−				
− −				
		_____	_____	_____
		+5	+11	+17*

Choosing Preferred Courses

For example, Tom calculated the impact of the various courses of action upon his overriding productivity value. The favorability levels were multiplied by the weighted value. Thus, "+ +" was converted to "+20," "+" to "+10" and 0 remained "0." As can be seen, the opportunities involved in the job change are most promising.

COURSES OF ACTION

VALUES	(Weights)	I Current Job	II Scheduled Promotion	III Job Change
Productivity	(10)			
+ +				+ + (+20)
+		+ (+10)		
0			0 (0)	
−				
− −				
		+10	0	+20*

Estimating Impact

In turn, Bill calculated the impact of the various courses upon his salary and time values. The favorability levels were multiplied by the weighted values and the columns were totaled. As can be seen, the job advancement appears most promising.

		COURSES OF ACTION		
VALUES		I	II	III
	(Weights)	Current Work	Overtime Work	Job Advancement
Productivity	(10)			
+ +				+ + (+20)
+			+ (+10)	
0		0 (0)		
−				
− −				
Time	(1)			
+ +				
+				
0		0 (0)		
−			− (− 1)	
− −				− − (− 2)
		0	+ 9	+18*

Estimating Multiple Impacts

John calculated the impact of the multiple courses upon his interpersonal performance and time investment values, and totaled the results. As can be seen, the interpersonal processing skill (**IPS**) training program appears to be most potent in terms of impacting his interpersonal performance and time investment values.

COURSES OF ACTION

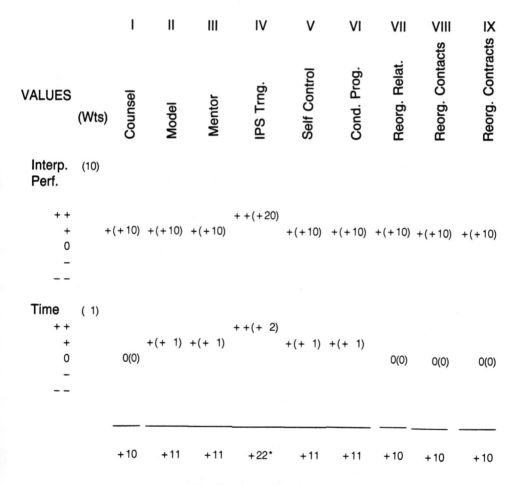

VALUES (Wts)	I Counsel	II Model	III Mentor	IV IPS Trng.	V Self Control	VI Cond. Prog.	VII Reorg. Relat.	VIII Reorg. Contacts	IX Reorg. Contracts
Interp. Perf. (10)									
+ +				+ +(+20)					
+	+(+10)	+(+10)	+(+10)		+(+10)	+(+10)	+(+10)	+(+10)	+(+10)
0									
−									
− −									
Time (1)									
+ +				+ +(+ 2)					
+		+(+ 1)	+(+ 1)		+(+ 1)	+(+ 1)			
0	0(0)							0(0)	0(0)
−									
− −									
	+10	+11	+11	+22*	+11	+11	+10	+10	+10

Multiplying Effects

Susan calculated the impact of her multiple courses upon her different values and sum-totaled the columns. As can be seen, the work/study course appeared most promising, in terms of impacting her values at the most favorable levels.

COURSES OF ACTION

VALUES	(Wts)	I Tutorial	II Counseling	III Career	IV Intern	V Culture	VI Work/Study
Skills	(10)	+(+10)	0(0)	0(0)	+ +(+20)	0(0)	+ +(+20)
Intellect	(9)	+(+ 9)	0(0)	0(0)	+(+ 9)	0(0)	+ +(+18)
Enjoyment	(5)	+(+ 5)	+(+5)	+(+5)	+(+ 5)	+ +(+10)	+ +(+10)
Motivation	(3)	+(+ 3)	+(+3)	+(+3)	+ +(+ 6)	0(0)	+ +(+ 6)
		+27	+8	+8	+40	+10	+54*

Sum-Totaling Effects

As a final example, Ann calculated the impact of her multiple courses upon her multiple values and sum-totaled the results. As can be seen, the housekeeper course appeared most potent for Ann's values.

COURSES OF ACTION

VALUES	(Wts)	I Continue Everything	II Babysitter	III Housekeeper	IV Time Training	V Perf. Plan.	VI Quit Job	VII Quit School	VIII Quit Everything
Children	(10)	−20	−20	+20*	+10	+10	+20	+10	+20
Husband	(9)	−18	+ 9	+18	+ 9	+ 9	+18	+ 9	+18
Professional	(8)	−16	+ 8	+ 8	+ 8	+ 8	−16	0	−16
Students	(7)	−14	+ 7	+ 7	+ 7	+ 7	0	−14	−14
Prof. Invest.	(5)	−10	+ 5	+ 5	+ 5	+ 5	−10	+ 5	−10
Home Invest.	(4)	− 8	− 4	− 4	+ 4	+ 4	+ 4	+ 4	− 8
Educ. Invest.	(3)	− 6	+ 3	+ 3	+ 3	+ 3	+ 3	− 6	− 6
Finc. Invest.	(1)	− 2	− 1	− 1			− 2		− 2
		−94	+ 7	+56*	+46	+46	+17	+ 8	−18

Choosing the Most Favorable Course

You may wish to apply your evaluation skills in choosing preferred courses of action. Selecting a simple problem and working alone, in pairs or in triads, you may apply the following steps: 1) weighting the values; 2) evaluating the impact; 3) choosing the preferred course.

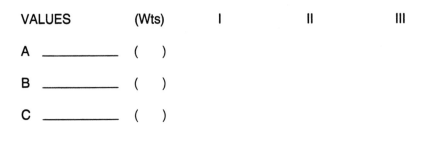

COURSES OF ACTION

VALUES	(Wts)	I	II	III
A _____	( )			
B _____	( )			
C _____	( )			

Applying Evaluation Skills

In summary, the preferred course of action is chosen based upon criteria indicating the most positive impact upon our values. We choose the preferred course by weighting the values, multiplying the weights times the favorability impact levels, and sum-totaling the results. Learning evaluation skills provides a quantitative method for evaluating the qualitative experiences of values.

Productive Evaluation Skills

7
IMPROVING
COURSES

Debbie had a problem. She always defined her values in "real" terms. Reality meant doing the things she had to do and investing the resources she had to invest. She could never tell what her "ideal" was and how close she came to achieving it. Then she learned a way of defining both ideal and "real" values in terms of the tasks she performed and the time she spent on each task. That way she could compare her real and ideal values, and upgrade the courses of action she chose.

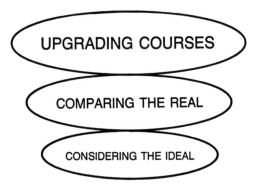

UPGRADING COURSES

COMPARING THE REAL

CONSIDERING THE IDEAL

Improving Courses

Considering the Ideal

There are some simple ways of considering "ideal" courses of action. An "ideal" course is what we would like to spend our time doing. It will provide us with a basis for comparison with our "real" courses, i.e., what we actually spend our time doing. Thus, we can calculate the effects of an ideal course by sum-totaling the products of the value weights and the most favorable levels (+ +). In other words, we can calculate what the total would be if an "ideal" course of action impacted all values at the most favorable level. In the example, Debbie's ideal course would be double the column total of the values weights, or, 32.

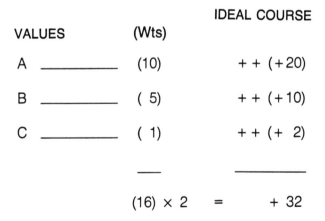

		IDEAL COURSE
VALUES	(Wts)	
A _____	(10)	+ + (+ 20)
B _____	(5)	+ + (+ 10)
C _____	(1)	+ + (+ 2)
	___	_____
	(16) × 2 =	+ 32

Considering the Ideal

For example, Tom has already found the ideal course to impact the most favorable level of his one overriding productivity value. In turn, Bill and John can both calculate the ideal total by multiplying the value weights by the most favorable level of impact (+ +) as follows:

$$11 \times 2 = 22 \longrightarrow \boxed{\text{Ideal Score}}$$

Similarly, Susan can calculate the ideal total by multiplying the total of her value's weights by a "double plus":

$$27 \times 2 = 54 \longrightarrow \boxed{\text{Ideal Score}}$$

Likewise, Ann can calculate her ideal total:

$$47 \times 2 = 94 \longrightarrow \boxed{\text{Ideal Score}}$$

Calculating Ideal Score

Comparing the Real

If the *ideal* course reflects how we would *ideally* like to spend our time, then the *real* course reflects how we *really* do spend our time. Armed with the total impact of the ideal course, we now have a basis for comparing the preferred course we have selected earlier. Thus, we can see that the ideal course total may be compared with the preferred course total in order to determine how closely our preferred course approximates the ideal. In the case of Debbie, the preferred course achieves approximately 63% of the value impact of the ideal course.

VALUES	(Wts)	IDEAL COURSE	PREFERRED COURSE
A _____	(10)	+ + (+20)	+ (+10)
B _____	(5)	+ + (+10)	+ + (+10)
C _____	(1)	+ + (+ 2)	0 (0)
	(16)	×2 = 32	+20

$$\frac{20}{32} = \boxed{63\%}$$

Comparing the Real

We can compare the real and the ideal value impact. For example, Tom had already achieved 100% of the ideal impact. In turn, Bill achieved a 82% level of ideal value satisfaction:

$$\frac{\text{Real}}{\text{Impact}} = \frac{18}{22} = \boxed{\text{82\% Ideal Impact}}$$

John achieved 100% of ideal impact:

$$\frac{\text{Real}}{\text{Impact}} = \frac{22}{22} = \boxed{\text{100\% Ideal Impact}}$$

Susan achieved 100% ideal value satisfaction:

$$\frac{\text{Real}}{\text{Impact}} = \frac{54}{54} = \boxed{\text{100\% Ideal Impact}}$$

Ann achieved only 60% of her potential ideal impact:

$$\frac{\text{Real}}{\text{Impact}} = \frac{56}{94} = \boxed{\text{60\% Ideal Impact}}$$

Calculating Percent of Ideal Impact

Upgrading Courses

We may or may not consider any of the ideal impact scores below 100% satisfactory. We always strive for the ideal. However, reality is a limiting and sometimes restricting factor. So we look for a rule-of-thumb. Under ordinary circumstances, 67% or ⅔ of the ideal value impact may be considered satisfactory. Usually, less than ⅔ requires an attempt to improve the course of action. Thus Debbie's ideal impact score of 63% is a borderline case. We may search among other courses of action for features to incorporate in order to upgrade the "ideal" course.

Ann's preferred course of action falls below two-thirds of ideal impact. Thus, we may set out to improve her preferred course. We can do this by first studying the deficits of the effects of the preferred course upon values. In so doing, we are seeking to examine any impact that is less than the most favorable (+ +) level.

COURSE III
Housekeeper

VALUES	(Wts)		
Children	(10)	+ +	
Husband	(9)	+ +	
Professional	(8)	+	
Students	(7)	+	
Prof. Invest.	(5)	+	Deficit
Deficit Home Invest.	(4)	-	Impact
Impact Educ. Invest.	(3)	+	
Finc. Invest.	(1)	−	

Evaluating Deficits

A primary source of improving the impact deficits involves studying the alternative courses of action. In so doing, we are looking for courses that could be incorporated into the preferred course of action. We can draw from any other sources that may improve the course. We may improve upon the preferred course by adding the following features: getting a personal tutor; getting a teacher's aide assigned; taking more vacation; reserving special family time; cutting down on school courseload; taking a loan. Of course, all new features may not be most highly favorable, but they do offer the potential of improving the ideal impact to 90%.

VALUES	(Wts)	COURSE III Housekeeper		IMPROVED COURSE III Housekeeper Plus	
Children	(10)	+ +		+ +	(+20)
Husband	(9)	+ +		+ +	(+18)
Professional	(8)	+	Tutor	+ +	(+16)
Students	(7)	+	Teacher's Aide	+ +	(+14)
Prof. Invest.	(5)	+	Vacations	+ +	(+10)
Deficit Home Invest.	(4)	−	Family Time	+	(+ 4)
Educ. Invest.	(3)	+	Cut Courseload	+	(+ 3)
Finc. Invest.	(1)	−	Loan	0	(0)

+ 85

$$\frac{85}{94} = \boxed{90\% \text{ Ideal Impact}}$$

Upgrading Deficits

Another method of improving courses is to incorporate non-exclusive complementary courses. In other words, we may incorporate any courses which are not mutually exclusive. In Ann's case, for example, she may add training programs in time management and performance planning. These programs have the potential of impacting the success of Ann's improved preferred course. Overall, these programs appear to have the most to contribute to Ann's values, and even these may be improved by incorporating other features.

VALUES	IMPROVED COURSE III Housekeeper Plus		COURSE IV Time Mgt. Training		COURSE V Perf. Planning Training	
Children	+ +	(+20)	+	(+10)	+	(+10)
Husband	+ +	(+18)	+	(+ 9)	+	(+ 9)
Professional	+ +	(+16)	+	(+ 8)	+	(+ 8)
Students	+ +	(+14)	+	(+ 7)	+	(+ 7)
Prof. Invest.	+ +	(+10)	+	(+ 5)	+	(+ 5)
Deficit Home Invest.	+	(+ 4)	+	(+ 4)	+	(+ 4)
Educ. Invest.	+	(+ 3)	+	(+ 3)	+	(+ 3)
Finc. Invest.	0	(0)	0	(0)	0	(0)
		+85		+46		+46

Complementing Courses

You may wish to apply your skills to improve the preferred course of action you have chosen. You may engage in the following activities: 1) calculate the ideal impact score; 2) compare the real with the ideal scores; 3) if less than 2/3 satisfaction of your values, then evaluate your deficits, incorporate features to improve your deficits and consider complementary courses of action.

1. CALCULATE   2. COMPARE   3. IMPROVE
    IDEAL   REAL   COURSES

Applying Improving Skills

In summary, improving preferred courses of action emphasizes incorporating features from other courses of action in order to compensate for deficits. We consider the ideal impact scores and compare the real impact scores. We upgrade the preferred course by incorporating features from other courses. Also, we complement the preferred course with facilitative courses that impact our values positively. Any course of action that satisfies our values less than fully may be improved upon provided we learn to live productively, i.e., constantly improving the efficiency of our resource investments and our results benefits.

Productive Improving Skills

8
PRODUCTIVE
PROBLEM
SOLVING

There are many different applications in problem-solving. There are applications in individual problem-solving such as we engaged in with Ann and others. Each of us may utilize the procedures which we have learned. We may solve problems in physical and intellectual as well as emotional areas just as Ann did.

There are also applications in group problem-solving. Groups may solve problems in much the same way that individuals do. We will attend to group problem-solving in detail in further works. Indeed, we may engage in organizational problem-solving at the highest levels. In so doing, we must understand the **PPS** skills and their impact.

PPS Skills

There is a great deal which participants and others can learn about themselves and their groups in the problem-solving process. The very act of developing the different stages yields knowledge about ourselves which may not have been clear beforehand. Certainly, the way we go about developing and breaking the problem down can tell us a great deal about how we experience pressure in our lives. But perhaps most important in terms of our new learning is how we develop the value hierarchy. What items we include or do not include, and how we define and weight them, tell us about what is present or absent in our lives, and to what degree. In addition, the process of considering and choosing courses of action informs us of how these values operate in relation to the different courses of action. In summary, the **PPS** process may tell us where we need improvement and where we are strong. We may apply it to real-life problems. It will guide our development in life.

First, and most important, we must be able to process the problem: attend to the critical sources of information; explore where we are in our experience; understand our goals for where we want or need to be in our experience. Recall the attending skills that facilitate involvement in **PPS**; the responding skills that facilitate exploring; the personalizing skills that facilitate understanding. Select a real-life problem to process.

Problem:

Second, we must be able to analyze the problem and synthesize the goal. We both analyze and synthesize in terms of the operational dimensions of phenomena. Recall the operational dimensions: components, functions, processes, conditions, standards. Apply your **PPS** analyzing skills to your real-life problem.

Problem: Goal:

Components

Functions

Processes

Conditions

Standards

PPS   Analyzing Skills

Third, we must be able to expand alternative courses of action to achieve the goal. Recall the expanding factors: people courses, program courses, organization courses. Apply your **PPS** expanding skills to your real-life problem.

Problem:

Goal:

Alternative Courses of Action

I	II	III	IV	V
"GO"				"NO GO"

PPS Expanding Skills

Fourth, we must be able to define our values in terms of their levels of favorability and/or productivity. Recall the use of time in defining observable and measurable dimensions. Apply these **PPS** defining skills to your real-life problem.

Problem:

Goal:

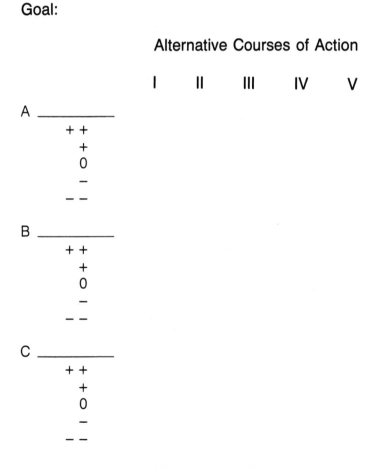

Alternative Courses of Action

	I	II	III	IV	V

A _____

++
+
0
−
− −

B _____

++
+
0
−
− −

C _____

++
+
0
−
− −

PPS   Defining Skills

Fifth, we must be able to evaluate the courses of action in terms of their impact upon our values. Recall weighting values, evaluating courses and choosing preferred courses of action. Apply the **PPS** evaluating skills to your real-life problem.

Problem:

Goal:

Alternative Courses of Action

VALUES	(Wts)	I	II	III	IV	V
A _____	( )	( )	( )	( )	( )	( )
+ +						
+						
0						
−						
− −						
B _____	( )	( )	( )	( )	( )	( )
+ +						
+						
0						
−						
− −						
C _____	( )	( )	( )	( )	( )	( )
+ +						
+						
0						
−						
− −						
		____	____	____	____	____
		( )	( )	( )	( )	( )

PPS   Evaluating Skills

Sixth and finally, we must be able to improve the preferred courses of action. Recall developing and comparing the ideal and real impact scores and upgrading the courses. Apply these **PPS** improving skills to your real-life problem.

Problem:

Goal:

VALUES	(Wts)	PREFERRED COURSE	IMPROVED COURSE	COMPLEMENTARY COURSES
A _____	( )	( )	( )	( )
++				
+				
0				
−				
− −				
B _____	( )	( )	( )	( )
++				
+				
0				
−				
−				
− −				
C _____	( )	( )	( )	( )
++				
+				
0				
−				
− −				
		( )	( )	( )

PPS Improving Skills

PPS Impact

Just as we train people in responsive and initiative dimensions in the emotional sphere of functioning, we can also train them in **PPS** skills. It is not enough to resolve problems. Ultimately, the individual or the group must be left with its own capacity for solving problems. This builds autonomy rather than dependency, and transforms people into helpers rather than helpless observers. In order to have this problem-solving capacity, people must be trained in the same **PPS** skills they have been offered. The problem-solving process is not complete until the individuals involved are equipped with the skills they need to solve their own problems.

The problem-solving process really represents the culmination of the helping process. It is only as good as the exploration and understanding phases that precede problem and goal definition and the development of the helpee's value hierarchy. And exploration and understanding phases are only as good as the helper's skills in responding to another person's experience. Our processing skills facilitate our **PPS** skills.

Exploring & Understanding ⟶ PPS

The development and implementation of any course of action, then, are only as good as the helper's skills in initiating from his or her own experience. In a very real sense, problem-solving involves the highest level of responsiveness of one human being to another, responding not just to a person's problems but to his or her need to be able to do something about problems. In this context, **PPS** skills facilitate personal action.

PPS ⟶ Action

In this regard, the problem-solving procedures may be used throughout life. Even the most fully functioning person may utilize the process to facilitate his decision making. For many people, a systematic problem-solving approach may become a way of life in which they can resolve conflicts, make choices, and develop directions that they might not otherwise have developed easily. Productive people constantly use **PPS** skills to manage important problems in their lives.

PPS as a Way of Life

Perhaps most important, **PPS** skills deliver results. They build in success every step of the way. They help to insure that the course of action chosen will be the one that most facilitates the things that the helpee values about achieving the goals involved. They insure to the highest probability that the goals achieved will resolve the problems the helpee began with.

PPS Benefits

Problems—large or small—are the responsibilities of individuals and groups—large and small. The degree to which we resolve them reflects the degree to which we emerge as effective and fully functioning persons and groups. In our communities and country today, many problems exist, at all levels, because we have not taken the responsibility for their resolution. Perhaps we have not taken the responsibility for their creation in the first place, and perhaps we have not had the **PPS** skills available to us in the second place. In any event, *we are responsible*. If we do not act to resolve the problems, we compound them.

PPS Skills

Each of us—as individuals or in groups—will encounter many problems in our lifetime. Productive people resolve their problems, and the price is hard work. Then they learn to solve the problems more and more effectively and efficiently. Non-productive people do not resolve them because that initial price seems too high. Perhaps the most distinguishing characteristic of productive vs. non-productive people is the determination and the ability to resolve their problems. Indeed, the most productive people invest themselves in a disciplined manner in doing everything possible to prevent the development of problems in the first place.

The choice is ours!

APPENDIX

(

PRODUCTIVE PROBLEM SOLVING OVERVIEW

1. Problem:

2. Goal:

3. Alternative Courses of Action

	I	II	III	IV	V	VI	VII	VIII	IX	X...
4. Values 5. Weights 6. Evaluate										

7. Column Totals

8. Preferred Course (*)

9. Ideal Score (2 × Weight Total)

10. Improve Course